DATE LOANED

CANYON UNION X X JAN 1 3 1971		
BASS X X AUG 2 3 1972		
MILLVILLE X X FEB 2 2 1973		
CEDAR CREEK X X SEP 2 8 1973		
HAPPY VALLEY 6 NOV 2 0 1974		
BASS X X MAR 1 6 1976		
CASTLE ROCK X X OCT 18 1977		
APR 2 5 1987		

GAYLORD 3563   PRINTED IN U.S.A.

The FIRST BOOK of FIJI

This Fijian belle, dressed for a party, wears a seashell hanging from a ribbon as a necklace, and has dabbed her cheeks and forehead with red paint as a decoration. (Photo: Rob Wright)

The FIRST BOOK of

FIJI

by Betty Cavanna

ILLUSTRATED WITH PHOTOGRAPHS

Franklin Watts, Inc.
575 Lexington Avenue
New York, N.Y. 10022

Cover photo: Huffman—Cushing

Library of Congress Catalog Card Number: 69-12389
71-2605 Copyright © 1969 by Franklin Watts, Inc.
Printed in the United States of America

1   2   3   4   5   6

Contents

The Beginnings of Fiji	1
The White Man Arrives	6
Cannibals	9
A British Colony	12
The Character of the Fiji Islands	14
The Larger Islands	15
People of Several Races	19
The Native Fijians	22
The Fijian Schools	29
The Fiji Language	32
Bau, Island of the Great Chiefs	32
The Indians in Fiji	36
Food in Fiji	40
Fijian Clothing	43
Sugar, Gold, and Coconuts	46
Sports and Amusements	49
The Yaqona Ceremony	53
The Fire Walkers	56
The Tourists Come	58
The Future of Fiji	62
Index	64

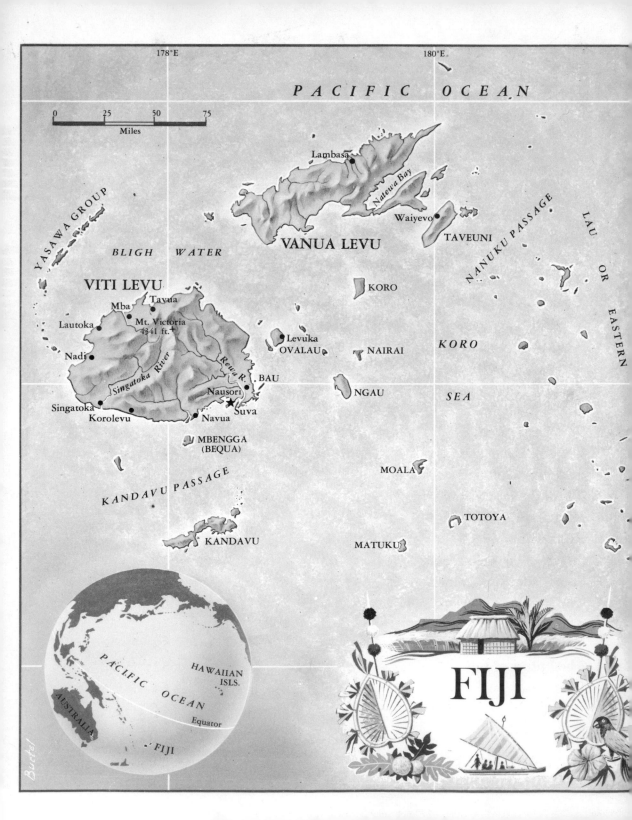

PACIFIC OCEAN

178°E   180°E

0   25   50   75
Miles

Lambasa

Natewa Bay

VANUA LEVU

Waiyevo

TAVEUNI

YASAWA GROUP

BLIGH WATER

NANUKU PASSAGE

LAU OR EASTERN

VITI LEVU

KORO

Mba   Tavua

Lautoka

Mt. Victoria
4341 ft.

Nadi

Singatoka River

Levuka
OVALAU

NAIRAI

KORO

Rewa R.

BAU

Nausori

Suva

Navua

Singatoka

Korolevu

NGAU

SEA

MBENGGA
(BEQUA)

MOALA

KANDAVU PASSAGE

TOTOYA

KANDAVU

MATUKU

PACIFIC OCEAN

HAWAIIAN
ISLS.

AUSTRALIA

Equator

FIJI

FIJI

Buchel

The Beginnings of Fiji

FIJI IS a group of islands lying in the southwest Pacific Ocean, about 1,100 miles north of New Zealand and about 1,200 miles south of the Equator. There are several hundred of these islands, dotted here and there over more than 100,000 square miles of sea. Some of them are large, but others are tiny. Only 106 of them are inhabited.

Some of these islands were formed millions of years ago when underwater volcanoes erupted and threw up great masses of lava and rock, which formed mountains high above the ocean's surface. In time, the sun and wind and rain acted on the rock and broke the top layers into small pieces. Gradually soil was formed from bits of rock. Seeds carried by seabirds and the ocean waters took root and grew. Little by little, wherever the hills were not impossibly steep, the islands became covered with trees and bushes and grass.

At the same time, billions of coral animals — tiny sea creatures — were building their colonies offshore wherever the water was shallow. As they died their limy skeletons formed walls of coral — barrier reefs — around many of the islands. The reefs then protected the land from all but the largest ocean waves. On the landside of the reefs, pools of quiet water called lagoons

1

were formed; they are now safe to swim in because dangerous fishes such as sharks cannot cross the barriers.

But not all the islands are surrounded by lagoons and reefs. Some have steep limestone cliffs exposed directly to the waves, which beat at them constantly and undercut them. On most of these islands only grass and a few half-starved trees and bushes have managed to gain a foothold.

In Fiji, this stretch of sandy beach is shaded with coconut palms and wild nut trees. (Photo: George Harrison)

Some of the smallest islands of all are made of coral limestone. A great number of these coral islands are atolls — circular rings of coral enclosing shallow pools, which are often broken open to the sea on the windward side. Some of the islands have so little soil that they are treeless; others have vines and grasses, and palm trees that have grown from coconuts brought in by the waves. Many of the coral islands rise less than ten feet above sea level and are almost completely awash at high tide.

After the islands of Fiji were formed, thousands and thousands of years went by before they were inhabited. Then people from Southeast Asia came in sailing canoes. They had island-hopped along a chain of land that led like a series of stepping-stones from the East Indies. These men and women planted crops to supplement the coconuts that were already growing on the islands and that were the main source of food and drink. The people settled down and raised families. They called their island home Viti, pronouncing the word somewhat as we say Fiji (FEE-gee) in English.

These first people to settle in the Fiji Islands, at about the time of Christ, were Melanesians who probably came from Papua, the eastern end of the island of New Guinea, which lies north of Australia. Their skin was very dark, almost black; their arms and legs were muscular; their hair was crisp and kinky.

They were experts at making canoes, which they built by scooping the center wood out of a tree trunk that had been pointed at both ends. Their small sailing canoes could skim swiftly through the water; their canoes for long-distance sailing had two large hulls fastened together by wooden crossties. On

3

Today's Fijians still sail double-hulled canoes like those of their ancestors. (Photo: Rob Wright)

the crossties a deck was built. It made a dry platform on which supplies could be carried well above the water. Some of these canoes were more than a hundred feet long, with tall masts for sails.

In time, Polynesian people from the islands of Tonga and Samoa came to trade with the Fijian people. They exchanged seeds and tools and other goods for boats in which they sailed back home. Some of the Polynesians — who were tall and well-built, with straight hair and rather fair, handsome features — stayed in the Fiji Islands and intermarried with the Melanesians. Gradually a people developed who were a mixture of the two races.

These are the people now known as the Fijis or the Fijians. They have characteristics of both the Pacific races from which their ancestors came. The Fijians have the quick intelligence of the Polynesians and the physical strength of the Melanesians. They are a happy and spontaneous people.

Their ancestors had learned the arts of both the Melanesians and the Polynesians. The Fijians became fine carpenters, and fishermen, weavers, potters, and farmers. For centuries they resisted the attempts of the white men to make them change their ways, for they had great force of character, and their code of behavior had been built up over thousands of years. Although they were savages and even cannibals until about a hundred years ago, they were clean and had quite a fine moral code.

A family group in a Fijian village today. The man at the right is wood carving; the woman second from the right is weaving a sleeping mat from palm leaves. (Photo: Huffman—Cushing)

The White Man Arrives

In 1643, the Fiji Islands were sighted by Abel Tasman, a Dutch explorer. He saw coral reefs in the distance, but sailed by without actually stopping, as navigation was difficult in the treacherous waters.

More than one hundred years went by before Captain James Cook stopped in 1774 at one of the smaller islands, now called Vatoa. Later, in 1789, shortly after the famous mutiny on the sailing ship *Bounty*, Captain William Bligh passed near the Fiji Islands during his long trip in an open boat in company with the men who had been set adrift with him.

Gradually British sailors learned to navigate the tricky channels between the islands. Soon adventurous sea captains arrived in search of sandalwood, gold, and spices; and traders came with cargoes of goods to barter with the natives. The waters of the islands were finally charted by an American expedition under Commander Charles Wilkes, in 1840.

In the early nineteenth century, hundreds of sandalwood trees were cut down by the Fijian people and were traded to sea captains for iron tools, guns, and rum. The heartwood of these trees is hard and fine-grained, and both the wood and the root contain a fragrant oil. Sandalwood was in great demand in China. Fans and boxes were carved from the sweet-smelling wood, and the oil extracted from the roots was used in making perfumes and medicines. When the supply of valuable timber began to run out in Fiji, a long, unhappy series of wars started among the Fijian people themselves.

Bunches of bêche-de-mer *hanging up, ready to be smoked. When cooked, these giant sea slugs produce a sort of gelatine. (Photo: Rob Wright)*

Then, in the 1820's, a new kind of trade developed with China. The people of Fiji learned to collect, cook, and dry large sea slugs called *bêche-de-mer*, the French words for "sea grubs." These slugs were covered with little bumps, and looked somewhat like long, thick dill pickles. They were prized as food by the Chinese.

Fijian divers gathered the slimy *bêche-de-mer* off the reefs of Fiji. The slugs were then boiled, split, and dried in a smokehouse until they were almost like leather. *Bêche-de-mer* took the place of sandalwood in the trade for guns, knives, and iron tools. A cargo of these dried slugs was valuable, and their exportation was a prosperous business for some years.

Some of the New England sailing ships made long voyages in several stages. In the trade with the islands of Fiji, a ship first took Yankee goods to South America, where they were sold for Spanish money. Next, the ship carried more of its cargo — iron

Tabua—*whales' teeth that are stained, oiled, polished, and fitted with cords by which they are handled. Weighing about a pound each, they are valued by the Fijians as gifts for special occasions. (Photo: Rob Wright)*

chisels and whales' teeth, among other things — to Fiji, where they were traded for *bêche-de-mer* for China. In China, the dried slugs were exchanged for chinaware, silks, and nankeen cloth, a durable, buff-colored Chinese cotton named after the city of Nanking, where it was made. All three of these Chinese products found a ready market in the United States at the end of the homeward voyage.

The Fijian people still have great reverence for *tabua* (tam-BOO-a), the teeth of the sperm whale, which they use as ceremonial presents on special occasions. The gift of one of these teeth is considered a great honor to the person who receives it. Ceremonial *tabuas* are often stained and smoked until they are a bright yellow. They are then polished to a brilliant sheen with coconut oil. No one is allowed to take *tabuas* out of Fiji without the consent of the local government.

Cannibals

AT ONE TIME the Fijian people were cannibals, who ate the flesh of enemies they had killed in war. Shipwrecked strangers were sometimes devoured as well.

Nobody knows how cannibalism first started. It may have developed in the distant past through some strange religious practice. In more recent times the Fijians ate *bokola*, "man-meat," because they believed they could in this way acquire the strength and valor of their victim. Cannibalism of this kind was a privileged practice of the chieftains. Eventually, over many centuries, Fijian men grew accustomed to eating the cooked flesh of human beings not because they wanted to be stronger or braver, but because they enjoyed the taste. Long before the first European landed on the islands, cannibalism had become mere greediness, and "long pig," or human flesh, had become a table luxury that few could resist. It is said that to satisfy his appetite a Fijian man would sometimes sacrifice even his friends and relatives.

Cannibalism in the Fiji Islands ceased not so very long ago. It is less than one hundred years since one old war chief became indignant when he could no longer get the human hearts and livers that had been his favorite food. His picture, a faded photograph showing him in full battle dress, still hangs in the council chamber on the island of Bau (m-BAH-u). His descendants tell of how he finally had to be sent to a small island where he could be kept alone, no longer a threat to the populace.

Christian missionaries helped put an end to cannibalism. The first missionaries, who came to the Fiji Islands in 1815, were Polynesian teachers from Tonga, an island group 600 miles to the east. They were followed by other missionaries from England and France and the United States.

Now the day when passing ships gave the cannibal islands of Fiji a wide berth is long past. The Fijian people still are great eaters, but they look back on their cannibal ancestors with a mixture of mild shame and amusement.

This Fijian, brandishing his war club, is showing how his ancestors looked in a war dance. He is wearing a grass skirt covered with a cloak of vines draped around his body. (Photo: Rob Wright)

The Parliament House in Suva, the capital of Fiji. (Photo: George Harrison)

A British Colony

THE ISLANDS of Fiji became a British colony voluntarily, not through being conquered in war. For a number of years two rival chiefs, Cakobau (kah-kom-BAH-oo) of the western islands, and Macafu (mah-KAH-foo) of the eastern, had struggled for power. Because neither was experienced in governing, each failed in his effort to establish a stable nation. It was with great relief that the people of Fiji learned, on October 10, 1874, that British Queen Victoria had finally agreed to accept dominion over the islands and to send out an English governor.

12

The new governor divided the islands into fourteen small areas called *yasanas* (provinces), and made use of Fijian customs and laws that were familiar and therefore seemed sensible and good to the natives. They settled down peaceably under British rule. Each *yasana* is administered by a chief called a *roko*; he is assisted by a provincial council that meets at least once a year.

Within the framework of the *yasanas* are seventy-six smaller administrative units called *tikinas* (districts), each controlled by a Fijian official called a *buli* (m-BOO-lee). He is helped by a *tikina* council that meets once a month.

A high chief stands in the door of the council chamber on the island of Bau. (Photo: George Harrison)

A still smaller unit is the *koro*, or village, of from fifty to one hundred people. There are more than one thousand villages in the islands. Each village has a lesser chief, and a local council concerned with collecting taxes, repairing roads, and looking after village health and sanitary problems.

Fiji has a constitution that provides for an executive council of ten men presided over by the governor, who is always appointed by the king or queen of England. The constitution was amended in 1963 to permit all adult island residents who can read and write to vote, no matter what their race.

The laws of Fiji, called ordinances, are made by a legislative council, also provided for in the constitution. The chairman of this council, called the speaker, is appointed by the Crown. He is the presiding officer of the forty legislative council members, thirty-six of whom are elected by the voters.

The Character of the Fiji Islands

ALL THE Fiji Islands together have a land area of a little more than 7,000 square miles. Although the larger islands are volcanic, none of the volcanoes is active.

Like most countries lying near the Equator, the Fiji Islands are hot and generally sunny. From November until March, when the sun is almost overhead at midday, the weather is very hot. During the rest of the year the climate is quite pleasant, with the temperature ranging between a high of 96° and a low of about 60° Fahrenheit. On the windward side of the high, volcanic islands the rainfall is heavy and there is often a thick forest. There is also plenty of water for raising crops. On the leeward side of the high islands, only plants that need little water can survive.

Ocean currents, rainfall, and winds greatly affect life on all these islands. While some of them have a good year-round climate, others are visited by terrible hurricanes. Storms come during the period between December and March. Each year there may be one or two dangerous ones that bring strong winds, heavy rains, and high, damaging tides. Then a whole island may tremble under the pounding of heavy seas. Sometimes the wind and waves sweep away all the people on a tiny island, even though they may have tied themselves high up in the palm trees.

One thing is certain. The Fijians are people of courage and resourcefulness. From earliest childhood, boys and girls are taught to understand and respect the sea. They know the danger, when a storm comes, of being caught outside the reef in a small canoe. But they also know how to open coconuts against a coral rock so that they can drink the milk and eat the nourishing meat as food if they are far from home and stranded, lost and hungry.

The Larger Islands

BY FAR THE biggest island in the Fiji group is Viti Levu (VEE-tee LEV-oo), which means "Great Fiji." It lies on the ocean path from Hawaii to Australia. Ninety miles long and about 65 miles wide from north to south, Viti Levu has an area of a little more than 4,000 square miles. The main Fijian industries are here, and so is the capital city, Suva. More than two-thirds of the entire Fijian population live on this island.

Suva, the largest city in the islands, has more than fifty thousand inhabitants. Like all large Fijian towns, it has an open-air market. Here, tradesmen sell farm-raised vegetables and fruit, sugarcane, baskets, pieces of coral, shells, cloth, necklaces, carvings, and tropical fish.

Mount Victoria, the highest mountain in Fiji, is on Viti Levu. It rises 4,341 feet above sea level. On the island there are also several rivers. Some of them are surprisingly large. The Rewa River is 90 miles long, and is wide and deep enough so that fairly large boats can navigate it for two-thirds of its length. Another river, the Singatoka, is 70 miles long. On the banks of each of these streams there are many small native villages.

Most of the plants on Viti Levu are tropical. Originally the rainy side of the island was covered with thick jungle — large trees draped with vines and orchids. Many of the plants are similar to those that grow in well-watered parts of Australia and New Zealand.

There are no large wild animals on Viti Levu or in the other islands of the Fiji group. A few nonpoisonous snakes are found. Sea turtles come to lay their eggs in the coral sand, and hermit crabs scurry along the beaches. Less interesting and pleasant are rats and bats; they are abundant.

There are many birds. Some of them, like the myna, were brought by people from India who came to live on the islands. The great albatross, called the king of the seaways, can occasionally be seen, and there are many terns and herons. Australian

Suva, the capital of Fiji, from the air. Ocean-going vessels lie at the docks in the foreground. (Photo: Rob Wright)

gray ducks are sometimes seen, and so are Fiji goshawks, peregrine falcons, fan-tailed cuckoos, and various species of rail, doves, and parrots. Among the songbirds are many species of flycatchers and warblers, and curious birds called white-eyes, which have a ring of white feathers around each eye.

To the northeast of Viti Levu lies Vanua Levu (van-oo-a LEV-oo), or "Great Land." Although it is only half as big as its sister island, Vanua Levu is still much larger than any of the other islands of the Fiji group.

Frigate birds and their young, Naido Island, Fiji. (Photo: American Museum of Natural History)

People of Several Races

IN ALL, about one-half million people live in Fiji. The islands are sometimes known as the "Little India of the Pacific," because Indians now outnumber the native Fijians.

Most of the Indians are Hindus or Muslims whose parents or grandparents were among some sixty thousand immigrants brought from India by the British between 1879 and 1916, to work in the sugarcane fields managed by Europeans.

Officials promised that eventually the newcomers would be given full citizenship and equal rights with the natives. The government also promised the Fijians that their land would not be taken away from them, however; it holds over 80 percent of the land in trust for the Fijians. To this day the native islanders refer to themselves as I Taukei (i tah-oo-KEH-i), or "landowners."

Most of the Indians who swarmed into Fiji were good and reliable workers. They were sadly disappointed in the living conditions on the sugar plantations where they were employed. The housing was poor, and there were no schools for their children until Muslim and Hindu missionaries arrived several years later to set up the beginnings of an educational system.

There was one bright spot in the situation. After each immigrant had served five years as an indentured laborer he was allowed to work for himself. Although some of the workers eventually returned to India, most of them stayed and rented small farms or went into business. At this point their lot became better in Fiji than at home, even though they had to lease their land from the natives and were not allowed to own it.

Indian people at a marketplace on Viti Levu. (Photo: Huffman—Cushing)

Today more than 90 percent of the people of Indian descent living in Fiji were born in the colony; their numbers are still increasing twice as fast as those of all other races. If an Indian can read and write, he is allowed to vote, but he wants to be able to own the land on which he lives or works. As long as the islands remain under British administration, however, the native Fijians will probably remain the owners, and the Indians will be the leaseholders.

In addition to the Fijians and the Indians there are a number of Europeans and people of mixed blood living in Fiji, and there are more than five thousand Chinese. These latter often work as shopkeepers and tradesmen. In the towns and cities the Chinese own most of the cafés, and nearly all the bread eaten in the islands is made in Chinese bakeries. There are many Chinese butchers, who sell meat shipped from overseas, as well as the beef and pork raised by Indian farmers. In trading with other islanders the Chinese speak the Fiji language, but among themselves many of them use the Chinese Cantonese dialect.

More than a thousand of the people living and working on Viti Levu are Rotumans. They came originally from an island group called Rotuma (ro-TOO-ma), which lies about 300 miles north of Viti Levu. Here the customs and language are somewhat like those of Samoa and Tonga, although Rotuma is a part of the Fiji archipelago.

In the towns about half the people are Indian, about a quarter are Fijian, and most of the others are European or part-European. Radio broadcasting stations in Suva send out programs in three languages. A daily newspaper is published in English, and weekly papers are printed in the Indian language Hindustani, and in Fiji.

The old and new styles in Fijian haircuts. (Photo: George Harrison)

The Native Fijians

IN LESS THAN one hundred years the Fijians have developed from the savages whom Charles Darwin called "people forever lost to civilization" to a forward-looking, adaptable group with a warmth and a hospitality that are endearing.

The typical Fijian man or woman is tall and well-built, with dark skin, a strong body, great dignity of bearing, and very thick hair, kinky and wiry enough to stand out in a self-supporting mop. Until quite recently it was fashionable for a person to let his hair grow long around his head in a bushy coiffure that added to his impressive appearance. This hairdress earned the Fijians the nick-name "mop-tops." Certain great chiefs formerly let their hair grow a foot long and dressed it in a great ball, often dyeing it with coral lime or tannin from mangrove bark, in colors ranging from solid bright red to wide white stripes. Today most Fijian people wear their hair in crew cuts only an inch or so long.

The Fijians are proud of their descent from a warrior race. Many of them are considerably more than six feet tall and are broad in proportion, as were their forefathers. The modern chiefs are real aristocrats. Usually they are handsome men of fine bearing and exceptional strength, and they are well educated. Many of them go to England for schooling, and to Oxford or Cambridge universities. They return to the islands with a mature understanding that education is important to their people if they are to compete with the more aggressive Indians in the islands.

Usually the Fijians are friendly and outgoing, even with strangers. If, at a *taralala*, a shuffle dance, a young girl sees a man who is attractive to her, she is likely to call out "Kasine!" (ka-SI-ne), meaning, "What a fine thing you are!" Sometimes she is even moved to make a neck-slicing gesture. This does not mean that she wants to kill him, but rather, it means "I'd cut my throat for you."

There are two Fijian characteristics that are rooted deep in the past, however, and that should not be forgotten. The tall, smiling Fijian man loafing on the outskirts of a ball field can turn into a deadly fighter, if need be. On Guadalcanal during World War II the Fijian soldiers became the terror of Japanese jungle fighters. Usually gentle, the Fijians can suddenly turn threatening.

23

And they have a feeling for tradition. They cling to their own way of life and prefer to live along the coast or beside a river in their ancestral thatch-roofed *bures* (m-BOO-res), or houses, rather than in cities. They raise enough food to live on, and they usually refuse to be lured by offers of steady employment. Rarely are they as industrious as the Indians, because manual labor does not appeal to them.

Even those Fijians who work in towns often go back at night to their own villages. This is natural, because the family is still the traditional unit of Fijian society. Each village is likely to consist mostly of members of a single family.

The local chief owes allegiance to the supreme chief of the tribe, who in turn owes allegiance to the king or queen of England through the Fiji government. Under a sort of clan system, property is owned in common by the whole community, and each village chief is like a strict but benevolent father. Under him, the workers hold a peculiar position, neither slave nor completely free. Each day the chief assigns certain duties to each villager. One group of people may be asked to pick coconuts, another to go fishing, and still others to mow the village lawn, to work in the vegetable gardens, or to join in building a home. This system encourages one person to help another.

Even if a Fijian man receives permission from the chief to leave his village to work in a city, he is still required to pay taxes at home — a home to which he may return each night, and also when he is old. So, the system offers social security to each Fijian person, for he knows that he will be cared for in his village in the final years of his life.

24

Most seashore or riverside Fijian villages are beautiful places to live in. Palm trees shade the thatch-roofed *bures*; turquoise-colored lagoons or silvery rivers lie offshore; a well-tended village green, bordered with bright flowers, surrounds a council house, which is usually built of wood and may have a thatched or a corrugated-iron roof. This "big house," as it is sometimes called, is the true center of village life. Here meetings are held, ceremonies are performed, and the treasures of the clan or tribe are kept. Visitors are always welcome to step inside the council house, and often the chief himself is on hand to show foreign travelers about. Sometimes church services are held here, although in most fair-sized villages there is a separate place of worship, just as there is a separate building for a school.

The Fijians today are among the tidiest people in the Pacific. The government annually offers a cash prize for the most attractive and best-kept village. Even though only one village can win, all of them try. Local pride is strong and every resident makes a personal effort to be clean and neat so that his village will always be in immaculate condition.

Most families have a plot of land big enough to hold a one- or two-room *bure*. The house has a timber frame often covered with a dense thatch of a reed grass called *gasau* (n-gah-SAH-oo). This way of building is sensible in a tropical climate, because the thatched roof and walls keep the inside of the house cool during the heat of the day.

The thatch is extremely thick, and as the roof must be kept waterproof, its material has to be repaired and replaced quite frequently. Long journeys may be needed to get the necessary

A village council house. (Photo: George Harrison)

A thatch-roofed Fijian house. In the background another house is under construction. (Photo: George Harrison)

reed grass. Nowadays some Fijians and most Indians use sheets of corrugated iron for roofing, because they last longer than thatch. These roofs rust quickly, however, and they are much less attractive than thatch, and not nearly so cool and pleasant.

The floors of the *bures* are usually covered with dried, long-leaved grasses. Over these are laid beautifully plaited mats that

A Fijian boy standing in front of a house whose walls are made of bamboo, split and woven. (Photo: George Harrison)

are comfortable to sit on cross-legged. The beams or walls of a house are often decorated with pictures of the British royal family and of illustrious Fijian people. The reeds forming the walls of the rooms are sometimes woven into colored designs, but this practice is becoming increasingly rare. A single wall of reeds usually separates the part of the house used as a bedroom from the one in which people eat and sit. The furniture is almost always primitive and scanty, since the Fijians spend most of their time outdoors.

Cooking is usually done in a small cookhouse containing an oven made of stones and clay. This house is shared by several families. Except for an earthen area where the fire is built, the floor of the cookhouse may be covered with mats and leaves. Frequently the fire is kept smoldering in order to smoke out mosquitoes and other insects.

The Fijians live under a traditional code called *kerekere* (ke-re-KE-re). According to the practices of *kerekere* a man must be willing to hand over to any of his friends or relatives anything that he owns. So, if a Fijian man opens a store, his sisters and cousins and aunts and friends consider themselves entitled to help themselves to merchandise off the shelves. Soon the poor shop owner faces bankruptcy. Anyone who refuses to follow the tradition of *kerekere* is likely to be ostracized in his village, which is mostly made up of his relatives. And when he himself needs help, he will not receive it. So, because of *kerekere*, it is almost impossible for Fijians to become successful money-makers.

A young Fijian mother with her children. (Photo: George Harrison)

The Fijian Schools

ALMOST ALL native Fijians speak some English, because they are taught that language in school, in addition to Fiji. Well-educated Fijians with university degrees from England or Australia speak the English language very fluently indeed. Many of these men and women hold important jobs in government, medical and health services, farming, education, business, missions, and the shipping industry.

The Fijians are usually anxious that their children be properly educated. They are always ready to help build a school or to give some of their land for a playing field. All Fijian boys and girls between the ages of six and fourteen are required to go to school, and those who show ability have a chance to get further special training for really important jobs. Sometimes boys and girls are taught in separate classrooms; sometimes together.

Schooling in Fiji is not free. Parents pay about twenty dollars for a three-term year for a child in the lower grades, and this fee increases as the child grows older. Children go to school from February to May, then have a two-week vacation. They go back to school until August, when there is another fortnight's recess,

Fijian schoolboys attending an outdoor class in Suva. (Photo: George Harrison)

then return until December, when the long summer holiday begins. Because Fiji is south of the Equator, summer comes there during what is winter in the northern hemisphere.

In many schools, children learn by rote, repeating sentences after their teacher until they are memorized. In some schools, radio broadcasts are used as a guide for English pronunciation. For instance, a fourth-grade class may be heard repeating after the broadcaster:

"The short man left his shoes in the ocean."

"Our queen is a good mother."

"Our queen visited Fiji in nineteen hundred and sixty-two."

All pupils wear school uniforms, which are neat and simple. The boys and girls seldom wear shoes until they reach the upper grades, when they adopt loose, comfortable sandals.

Young island boys of exceptional intelligence and ability are occasionally selected to go on to Suva's Central Medical School, to study medicine. There, in a five-year course, they meet other young students brought to Suva from nearly every major island group in the South Pacific. Barefoot, bare-legged, and dressed in simple native style, the boys attend classes that teach them the white man's medical knowledge and skills, but discourage them from acquiring his habits. The institution's aim is to send able young doctors back to their own people, but to keep them as simple in manner as when they entered the school.

Funds from the Rockefeller Foundation are now making it possible to enlarge the school, and each year more graduates of ability — surgeons as well as medical men — are saving the lives of people in remote areas of the Pacific.

The Fiji Language

IT WAS THE missionaries who first provided Fiji with a written language. To do this, they had to develop an alphabet. They used the English letters, but changed their pronunciation to suit the Fijian way of speaking. Fiji is hard to imitate with English letters. The missionaries solved this problem by assigning to some single letters the sound of two letters. For instance, the letter "d" sounds like "nd"; the letter "b," like "mb"; and the letter "g," like "ng." Therefore the town spelled Nadi in Fiji is pronounced NAN-di; the island spelled Bau is pronounced m-BAH-oo; Deuba is pronounced n-de-OOM-ba. English geographies and gazetteers often add the missing letters. In the Fiji language every vowel is sounded.

Thirty different dialects are used in the Fiji Islands, but the official language is that used on the island of Bau.

Bau, Island of the Great Chiefs

FROM THE AIR the historic island of Bau looks like a big pancake resting on the gray-blue water just off the shore of Viti Levu. It is formed chiefly of soapstone and is fringed with mangrove trees. At high tide, Bau is a short pull from Viti Levu by rowboat, but at low tide, people often trudge barefoot through ankle-deep mud from the big island to the little one.

Bau covers only 20 acres. It is one of the smallest islands lying

32

The island of Bau, famous home of Fiji chiefs. (Photo: George Harrison)

off Viti Levu, yet it is easily the most important. For centuries it has been the birthplace and home of Fijian chiefs.

Early in the nineteenth century, when there were many kings in the Fiji Islands, all warring one with another, the people of Bau began to build huge war canoes and extend their chief's influence by raiding distant islands. Because the little kingdom was small and insignificant, its rulers had to be very clever and brave to survive. This they were. By the 1830's, the chief of Bau had conquered many of the western islands of Fiji. He maintained a large fleet of war canoes, along with two hundred small canoes, which brought tribute and supplies to Bau's more than three thousand inhabitants.

One of the early chiefs selected eight principal wives from his various domains, but the wife from Bau itself was the mother of the great chief Cakobau. In 1854, Cakobau, by then the most powerful chief in the islands, became a Christian, and thousands of the Fijian people followed him into the new faith. But in the eastern islands the Tongan prince called Macafu was a serious rival. For years there were two separate governments, one in the east and one in the west. In time, however, Cakobau pronounced himself *Tui Viti*, or chief of all Fiji, and proclaimed Bau his capital. Like his ancestors, many of his descendants were born on the island.

Bau contains three small Fijian villages — one called Bau, which is the home of the high chiefs; another called Soso, which is the home of craftsmen; and another called Lasakau (lah-sa-KAH-oo), which is the home of fishermen. Altogether, the three villages now contain only about three hundred people.

In the center of a clipped green lawn in the major village of Bau stands a large monkeypod tree, and in the center of a circle of *bures* is a big council house. This building is raised high off the ground on a terraced foundation said to have been the site of an ancient temple. At the southern end of the green is the Cakobau Memorial Church, and on a knoll fifty feet higher up is an airy village schoolhouse.

Flowers bloom all around, and carefully tended vegetable gardens grow near the shore. In a burial ground up beyond the school, high above this peaceful scene, lie members of the Cakobau family, resting in state on the island of great chiefs.

Bau is one of the few small areas of Fiji where residents still make their own rules about their way of living. The people have

Children coming down from their schoolhouse on the island of Bau.
(Photo: George Harrison)

their own council, which has the power to collect taxes from everyone living or working on the island. These funds are supplemented each year by a sum from the Fiji government. The money is spent on roads, sanitation, and medicine, for the benefit of the people of the island.

The Indians in Fiji

THE INDIAN Hindus and Muslims can easily be distinguished from the Fijian people, as their hair is straighter and most of them are slighter in build. It is also easy to tell an Indian settlement

While her family gathers around her, this Indian woman is grinding coconut, using a wooden pounder. (Photo: Huffman — Cushing)

from a Fijian village, for Indian houses are usually built of rough timber and sheet iron, and look dreary and ordinary in comparison with the attractive Fijian *bures*. Furthermore, the Indians usually settle along roads and railways on good farmland, instead of near water. They often build their houses on high land that cannot be flooded during heavy rains. They are content with a few trees for shelter or for fruit-bearing, and generally do not care how neglected and ill-kept their yards may appear.

The Indians work hard, however. It is the Indian farmers who supply the city, town, and village markets with rice, maize, beans, pineapples, tapioca, peanuts, taro, goat meat, beef, and tobacco. They carry their crops to market by road or river and take their sugarcane to the mills by railway.

This Indian surf fisherman at Singatoka, in Fiji, wears a traditional turban. (Photo: Huffman — Cushing)

Those Indians who do not like farming often become store-keepers or businessmen. In Fiji there are Indian building contractors, importing and exporting firms, wholesale and retail shops, tailors, and shoemakers. Nearly all transport services are owned by Indian firms, as are most of the motion-picture houses. Since the Indians are ambitious, many of them have become prosperous through banking. Few of them have taken advantage of a government guarantee of free passage back home, for in India they would now be considered foreigners and outcastes. In the islands, however, they keep their national character. A number of the men still wear beards and turbans, although most of them favor clothes made in the European fashion. The women usually dress in their native *saris*.

Very few Indians speak Fiji. For a long time they made themselves understood in the islands by means of a simple dialect called Fiji-bat. But nowadays many of their young people use the English they have been taught in school. Most of the older people still speak Hindustani, which is understood by nearly all the Indians. But in small groups whose relatives have come from the same district in India, people almost always use the language that was spoken in that region.

Although the Indians may live near the island natives, there is little mingling between the two groups. Both may speak English, but it is still a foreign language, and most persons cling to their native tongue.

The difference in languages makes a barrier between the two races that only education can lessen. Unfortunately, education for Indian children is not compulsory in Fiji. There are mission

An Indian temple at Lautoka, in Fiji. (Photo: Huffman—Cushing)

schools for them, but since the small farms are usually worked by two adults with some help from their children, many young people are forced to make do with very little learning indeed. In Fiji a great many Indian children, especially girls, cannot read or write. In one part of the capital city of Suva, twenty thousand Indians live in an area a mile square. If school segregation of Fijians and Indians could be done away with, all the islanders would benefit.

39

Food in Fiji

IN THE EARLY days of the islands, the Fijians lived mainly on fish and coconuts. For a starchy food they used a large round fruit with a whitish pulp, whose consistency was that of fresh bread. This breadfruit, so called, which grew on trees native to the islands, could be mashed, fermented, and kept in a pit for years, to be cooked as needed. Today, of course, the Fijian diet is more varied, but it still contains a number of foods that are strange to many outsiders.

Among these Fijian foods are two plants that are raised in large quantities. One, called *dalo* (n-DAH-lo), is more commonly known as taro; the two words were originally the same. *Dalo*

An Indian merchant selling taro root in a marketplace. (Photo: George Harrison)

An open-air market in Suva. In this stall a Fijian farmer is selling bananas, coconuts, taro root, turnips, squash, and many other fruits and vegetables. Some of them are contained in baskets made from plaited palm fronds. (Photo: George Harrison)

grows well in wet land. It takes nearly a year to mature, and forms a large root that, when baked, is starchy and nourishing. The other plant is manioc, or cassava, which has a fleshy root used in making tapioca flour. A kind of bread called *mandrai* (man-DRA-i) is made from the *dalo* root and also from yams, which are somewhat like big sweet potatoes.

The natives ordinarily have only two meals a day. They cook in earth and stone ovens and eat out of pots with their fingers, instead of using knives and forks. Etiquette in a Fijian village

41

requires that foreign visitors eat first; chiefs and men of rank eat next; and women and children eat what is left over. Since Fijians are ceremonious people, mealtime in the *bure* of a chief usually finds him eating alone or with masculine guests. He is served by a waiter who enters the dining room on his knees, according to long-established custom.

A typical feast may consist of mussel soup; baked fish or turtle meat; suckling pig roasted on hot stones; fried bananas; breadfruit in the creamy juice of a not quite ripe coconut; chicken baked in banana leaves; and perhaps crabs, shrimps, and oysters.

Humpbacked Indian oxen are used as draft animals in the sugarcane fields. (Photo: Huffman—Cushing)

There may also be sweet potatoes and yams; manioc; pineapple pudding; and a tea made from lemongrass and from a kind of leaf that is lemon-flavored. One of the great delicacies enjoyed by the Fijians is cooked *balolo* (m-ba-LO-lo), a sca worm that can be scooped in great numbers from the lagoons each autumn at a particular time.

Many cattle are raised in Fiji for their meat and hides and also for drawing plows. The working animals are a cross between cattle imported from Australia and elsewhere, and zebus, humpbacked cattle brought originally from India. Zebus are well able to bear tropical heat. Although Fijian beef is rather tough, it is tasty and nourishing.

The Indian inhabitants of Fiji eat their own national foods. Their principal staple is rice, which they raise in large quantities. Many of the Indians look down on the native Fijians as eaters of undesirable meats. (Followers of the Hindu religion do not eat beef, and followers of the Muslim religion do not eat pork.)

Fijian Clothing

ALTHOUGH TODAY many Fijian men wear European clothes, most of them still wear a wraparound skirt called a *sulu*. Made of gray or brown cotton or light wool, this garment ends slightly below the knee, and is worn with a conventional white shirt and necktie, and with sandals. At times the climate in Fiji is rather humid, and a *sulu* is much cooler to wear than a pair of trousers. It rains fairly often in the hot wet season, and most people carry

43

Fijian men in typical garb — sulu *and white shirt. (Photo: George Harrison)*

umbrellas instead of wearing raincoats, since the coats are too warm.

A soldier or a policeman wears a *sulu* with a different hemline than usual. This *sulu* is cut in a series of points, and the shirt worn with it is sometimes colored. A sentry standing guard before a government building looks very impressive in his long *sulu,* broad red cummerbund, or sash, and black shirt.

While the younger Fijian women have adopted European short

skirts, the older ones wear bright printed cottons that are usually a short dress over a long skirt. Before the missionaries arrived, the women wore brief wraparound garments somewhat like *sulus*. Under missionary influence these garments became long petticoats over which the wearers put flowered outer frocks that came slightly below the knees. The older women still cling to this style.

For special ceremonies the Fijians often wear costumes resembling those of their ancestors. These costumes were made of grass, leaves, and tapa cloth. This cloth is not woven, but is beaten from the bark of the paper mulberry tree. A piece of suitable bark is soaked in water and then pounded thin with a heavy stone. It takes many hours of work to pound out enough thin bark for a dress. Pieces of cloth are joined by being pounded together before

A Fijian soldier on sentry go before the governor's mansion in Suva. On the gatepost is the British coat of arms. (Photo: George Harrison)

they are quite finished. In the process the fibers of the two pieces become so entangled that a single length of fabric results.

After the creamy-white or light-brown tapa cloth has been dried in the sun, plant juices are used to stain it in intricate patterns of brown or black. Traditional freehand designs are painted on the cloth, or they may be transferred to the fabric by rubbing it while holding it against stained wood carvings. Although the colors used are rather dull, the designs are often striking.

Besides being used to make clothes, bark cloth is frequently used to decorate the inside walls of houses. Pieces of carefully made tapa cloth make highly prized wedding presents.

Sugar, Gold, and Coconuts

TODAY'S FIJIAN people need many things that must be imported from the outside world. To pay for these goods, the islanders must have products to export and sell. The three principal cargoes taken from Fiji are sugar, coconut oil, and gold. The Fijian people also export, mainly to Australia and New Zealand, cocoa beans, bananas, pineapples, ginger, hides, tobacco, and seashells.

Coconut trees were growing on most of the islands when the first people arrived. When white men came, great plantations of these trees were set out. The dried white meat of the coconut, called copra, is in demand in the outside world for making soap, margarine, and many other products. Today, Fiji exports fewer tons of copra each year than formerly, but copra still remains an important product.

46

In the 1930's, rock containing flecks of gold was found in the islands, and several fairly rich goldfields have been mined ever since. One of the most important is at Tavua in northern Viti Levu. There are also gold mines at Batakula. The mining companies are owned by Australians. They employ several hundred Fijian and part-European miners to dig the ore and crush it by machinery to obtain the grains of gold. Another mineral, manganese, is also mined in Fiji.

The most important export today is sugar. Much of the 83 percent of land owned communally by the Fijian natives is leased to Indian farmers who raise sugarcane on it. A large corporation called the Colonial Sugar Refining Company buys the cane and operates mills in which it is crushed. Its juice is extracted and boiled down until only brown sugar mixed with molasses is left. This mixture is refined to make various grades of granulated sugar.

The sugar company, which has its headquarters in Sydney, Australia, helps the Indian cane farmers by giving advice about the best kind of cane to grow in order to get large crops, and the best way to prepare the land where sugarcane is grown. Most of the Europeans who are employed in Fiji work for this company.

There are few factories in the islands. A great many of the village people support themselves by working with copra, by fishing, by gathering seashells and sea slugs, by digging valuable roots, or by harvesting such fruits as bananas or breadfruit.

In recent years many farmers have planted cacao trees. When these trees are young, they have to be sheltered from the sun by rows of banana trees or other quick-growing tropical plants. After

47

Sacks of dried copra being loaded on an interisland freighter in Fiji, for transportation to Suva, where oil will be pressed from the coconut meat. (Photo: Rob Wright)

A view of a gold-mining operation in Fiji, photographed at dusk. (Photo: Rob Wright)

the cacao plants are about eight years old, they produce pods that are filled with beans. These beans are cured and then are shipped overseas, where they are roasted and crushed into the brown powder used in making cocoa or chocolate. Various drugs and medicines are also made from parts of the cacao tree.

Sports and Amusements

BOTH THE Fijian people and the Indians are football enthusiasts, and Sunday games are popular. The Fijians are said to prefer the English game called Rugby; and the Indians, soccer. But both races play both games, and their teams often compete. Baseball is not played in the islands. Instead, both the Fijian people and the Indians, like most people with British connections, are fond of cricket, a game played with balls, bats, and wickets, by teams with eleven men on a side.

Big crowds turn out for the cricket and football games. The spectators fill the reserved seats in the grandstands, and line the sides of the field six deep, cheering for their teams. Mothers with nursing babies sit on the outskirts; children are carried high on their fathers' shoulders; and peddlers push carts of food and soft drinks through the throng.

The Fijian natives are more fun-loving than the Indians, but they are also rougher. They usually play football barefoot, and when they play an International Match with a team of Maori from New Zealand, excitement runs high.

Fijians surrounding a school of fish with a net. (Photo: Rob Wright)

The Fijians often have fish drives which, although held primarily for gathering food, are the occasion for much sport. Using nets as long as a football field, which they weave from long vines tied together, they attempt to encircle a school of fish in shallow water. If frightened too much, the fish could easily escape, so the natives pour certain plant juices into the water. These juices drug the fish, which can then be easily speared and caught.

On sunny days between March and October, boats are often

50

taken out beyond the reefs to catch sea turtles. The flesh of these turtles is most delicious to eat, and their shells are valuable in world markets.

The Fijian people are usually good swimmers, because most of them have grown up either beside the sea or along a riverbank. They do not often think of water as a place for sports, however. When they sail or row a boat, it is to get from one place to another. When they fish, it is to catch food. Only around the main ports like Suva do some people enjoy water sports.

The birthday of the British monarch is always celebrated in Fiji with a parade, either in Suva or in Lautoka (lah-oo-TO-ka), the second largest city on Viti Levu. And schoolchildren always have a holiday on May 24, the birthday of Queen Victoria, who was ruler when Fiji joined the British Empire.

Fijian dancing, except among a few westernized young people, is of the ceremonial or traditional type. In dances called *mekes* (MEK-ez) historical legends are portrayed. *Meke-wesi* (MEK-e WEZ-i) is a frenzied stamping dance with spears and war clubs — a former prebattle routine performed by men smeared with coconut oil and war paint, and wearing leaves and streamers. The men look extremely fierce and dance with great concentration, acting out the violence with which one tribe made war on another.

A spear-and-fan dance is also popular. This is another rhythmic stomp, punctuated by bamboo-spear thumps and the drawing of fans across the teeth of the performers. A *vaka malolo* (VAH-ka ma-LO-lo) is a sitting *meke* done by women whose swaying bodies and graceful arm-and-finger pantomimes keep time to a musical chant.

51

In this ceremonial war dance the warriors, dressed in skirts made of pandanus leaves, brandish their war spears fiercely, while chanting to the beat of drums. (Photo: Rob Wright)

Group singing is especially enjoyed by Fijian women. Many of their songs are based on the old Methodist hymns brought by early missionaries from the United States. Every Sunday evening, at Suva's Methodist Centenary Church, a 150-voice Fijian choir draws visitors from far and near. Many present-day Fijians are steadfast believers in the Methodist faith, and church-going occupies an important place in their lives. Some attend all of the four services held on Sundays, and also go to church on Wednesday and Saturday mornings. The church programs are almost always dominated by boisterous hymn singing.

The Yaqona Ceremony

Yaqona (yan-GO-na) is the Fijian word for a drink called *kava* elsewhere in the South Sea area. It is made from the roots of a large pepper plant. The roots are first dried in the sun and are then pounded to powder. This powder is added to cold water in a wooden bowl, and the mixture is either squeezed through a muslin cloth or strained through a skein of hibiscus stems. The resulting drink is not alcoholic, but is slightly narcotic, with an

A chief squeezes out the liquid to be drunk at the yaqona *ceremony. (Photo: Rob Wright)*

Fijian women dance at a yaqona *ceremony. (Photo: George Harrison)*

astringent effect that is a little bit numbing to the mouth and tongue.

Yaqona is served as a welcome to honored guests. For hundreds of years the traditional *yaqona* ceremony of welcome has been a formal rite in Fiji.

Usually in this ceremony, male dancers dressed in skirts made from the leaves of a pandanus tree, and with their faces blackened in designs of soot from a burned coconut, perform a whirling ritual dance. An accompanying chorus of women wearing costumes of tapa cloth sings ancient chants.

Until modern times the beverage was made by a group of young women who chewed the roots and spat the juice into a bowl where, after the addition of a little water, it was allowed to ferment. Today more sanitary methods are used to make *yaqona*, but the drinking ceremony remains the same.

Usually a village chief has the honor of making the *yaqona* in a large wooden bowl. He pours water from a gourd as he sifts the powder through his hands. Each movement he makes in removing particles of root from the juice is performed in a traditional manner. When the drink is ready, the chief cries *"Talo!"* (meaning "Serve!") as he fills a cup made from a coconut shell.

The guest of highest importance is given the first cup as a token of friendship and goodwill. The cupbearer kneels, facing the recipient, and holds the cup before him with outstretched arms. There is complete silence as the visitor empties the cup in a series of gulps. When he returns it, the Fijian hosts chant *"Maca,"* which means "The cup is drained."

The cup is then spun on the ground like a top, to show that it is empty. The ceremony is repeated as the second most important guest is given a drink. Then the third most important guest receives the cup, and so on, until all the honored guests have been served.

The *yaqona* ceremony is always dignified and reverent. It is a tradition cherished by the Fijian people. Usually more dances follow it. Then a feast is served on fresh green leaves and is eaten in the Fijian manner, with the fingers.

The Fire Walkers

ON A BEAUTIFUL, mountainous island called Bequa (m-BENG-ga), which is south of Viti Levu and can be approached from it only across a deep channel, there lives in one village a group of men who can walk barefoot on red-hot stones without being burned.

There are many legends of this island, which is called the "Holy Land" of Fiji. One story tells of a great flood much like that recorded in the Bible. The survivors of this flood are said to have landed on top of a mountain on Bequa and to have gone back later to resettle the whole of Fiji. Another legend is that of how the women from a village called Kandavu were given the skill of calling turtles out of the sea. It is said that the women of Kandavu still have this ability. Still another legend of the island tells how a god gave a human being the ability to walk on very hot stones.

Visitors to Bequa can still occasionally witness a fire-walking ceremony. First, a pit about four feet deep and fifteen feet across is dug to form a fireplace. The pit is piled full of large logs that are set on lava rock or on the large stones from a riverbed. The logs are set afire, and when the blaze is very hot, boulders are piled onto it. Within a day or so, the boulders begin to explode from the heat, and the whole furnace reaches so high a temperature that an onlooker cannot approach within ten feet of it. Then the ashes are raked away to expose the hot stones.

Now a witch doctor leads the fire walkers in a religious procession through a bed of wet sand. After this, they walk leisurely over the searing stones. Although the *sulus* of the fire walkers are

Fijians walking on red-hot stones, in the fire-walking ceremony. (Photo: Rob Wright)

often singed, there is no trace of burning on the thick-skinned soles of their feet.

Various explanations of this unusual circumstance have been given, but each is probably only a partial explanation. One is that the natives, accustomed to walking barefoot a great deal, have such thick callouses on the bottoms of their feet that they are insensitive to pain. They are often able to stick pins one-quarter of an inch into their soles without feeling the stab.

Another explanation is that the soles of the fire walkers' feet are moist from walking through the wet sand, and a thin layer of steam forms as soon as the walkers step on the hot stones. Not much heat can cross this barrier of steam.

The Tourists Come

TODAY ONE of the principal businesses in Fiji is the entertainment of tourists, who come from all over the world. Jet airplanes can bring travelers quickly and easily to these formerly remote islands, which are now only twelve hours by air from San Francisco.

On Viti Levu there are several good hotels, which are usually filled with tourists who have stopped off for a few days on their way to the United States, Australia, or New Zealand. Visitors are frequently surprised to find so up-to-date a place. A car can be rented as easily in a large town on Viti Levu as in any American city, and larger towns have the conveniences of modern living — telephones, electricity, and running water.

A street corner in the business district of Suva. (Photo: Rob Wright)

A tall, husky policeman passes a group of taxi drivers on a street in Suva. (Photo: George Harrison)

The islands have their own system of money. Although it is reckoned in pounds, shillings, and pence, as in the British monetary system, its values are not the same.

The paper money is printed with pictures of sea turtles and sailing canoes, with the British monarch's head on one side of the bill and that of a prominent Fijian on the other. Fiji also issues its own postage stamps, which are in great demand by collectors.

A narrow-gauge railroad runs across part of the island of Viti Levu, crossing the area on which sugarcane is grown. The tiny locomotive pulls a long train of small cars loaded with cane on its way to the crushing mills. The license given the railroad when it was first installed in 1915 specified that anyone who wished to ride on the train must be carried free, provided he would jump off at his own risk whether the train was moving or not as it reached his destination. Jumping off is not as dangerous as it sounds, for the little train moves slowly across the countryside. Many tourists ride the 112 miles from Lautoka to Kavanagsau (kav-an-ang-SAH-oo) on one day, then take the train back on the next day. Or a person can spend about nine hours on the round trip to the sugar mills and back to Rarawai (rah-ah-WAH-i).

Because of tourist interest in Fijian customs, the ancient ceremonies are held more often now than they would otherwise be.

Old Fijian drums called *lali*, made of hollowed tree trunks, were formerly used to warn a tribe of a threatened attack or to summon people to ceremonies or religious meetings. These drums make a dull, booming sound when struck with wooden hammers. Now they signal mealtimes in some resort hotels, besides being used to call people to church.

A Fijian drummer with his drum made from a hollowed log. (Photo: Rob Wright)

Few tourists leave Fiji without taking along some samples of the Fijian arts and crafts. Bowls and plates carved from the wood of the monkeypod tree are in great demand by tourists, and so are models of war canoes and clubs.

Because much of the main island is ringed by mud flats, few beaches are attractive to swimmers. One of the few good swimming beaches is at Korelevu (koh-re-LEV-oo). Because this is inside a coral reef, there is good underwater scenery for skin divers. During the rainy season, from December to March, the water at most of the beaches is likely to be muddy; it is fairly clear from May to October.

Many seashells are found in Fijian waters, and island divers still turn up an occasional golden cowrie shell, a good specimen of which may be worth from fifty to one hundred dollars.

Vacationists can travel among the outer islands on small ships, most of which carry about a dozen passengers. There are also interisland cargo ships that pick up copra at little-known ports where natives live in much the same manner as they did a thousand years ago. These ships make trips of about a week's duration, and touch at such spots as Levuka, Savasavu, Taveuni, Butha Bay, and Rambi, well off the beaten tourist path.

The Future of Fiji

INTEGRATION IS the big problem in Fiji today. The Indians and the native Fijian people are very different in temperament, and are separated by language, by religion, and by the property laws.

Their children go to separate schools, and their families tend to congregate in separate areas of each island.

Indian leaders are eager for their people to own land rather than merely rent it. They keep reminding British officials that the Indians were originally attracted as laborers to the islands by promises that were not kept. They point out that, without the efforts of the hardworking Indians, Fiji's whole economic structure would soon collapse.

The Fijians, on the other hand, feel that the islands and all the land on them are theirs, and point out that they were promised that none of these lands would ever be sold. They tend to resent the competition given them by the Indians, who are usually more interested in financial success than the Fijians are.

Much trouble has arisen because of these conflicting promises made by a former government that wished to build up the Fiji economy by importing laborers. Today a new generation of progressive-minded Fijians and Indians is studying the rights of both communities. Many businesses are making a point of employing Fijians, Indians, and Europeans without discrimination. The latter group is providing money to start new industries, while the Fijians have made more of their land available for rental to Indians.

Most experts agree, however, that these efforts are scarcely keeping pace with the problem. They feel that the native Fijian people must give up more of their social customs and communal living and become more aggressive workers, farmers, and businessmen if they are to survive economically.

Index

Animals, 16, 18, 43
Atolls, 3

Balolo, 43
Barrier reefs, 1-2
Bau, 10, 32, 34-36
Beaches, 62
Bêche-de-mer, 7-8, 9
Bequa, 56
Birds, 16, 18
Bligh, Captain William, 6
Bokola, 9
Breadfruit, 40
British monarch, 14, 24
Buli, 13
Bures, 24, 25, 27-28

Cacao, 47-48
Cakobau, 12, 34, 35
Cannibalism, 9-10
Canoes, sailing, 3-4
Cassava, 41
Cattle, 43
Chiefs, Fijian, 10, 23, 24, 34, 42, 55
China
   trade with, 6, 7, 8, 9
Chinese, 21
Church-going, 52
Clan system, 24
Climate, 14-15, 43-44

Clothing
   Fijian, 43-46
   Indian, 38
Coconuts, 3, 15, 40, 46
Cook, Captain James, 6
Cooking, 28
Copra, 46
Coral, 1, 3
Council house, 25, 35
Councils, Fijian, 13, 14
Cricket, 49
Crops, 37, 46, 47, 49

Dalo, 40-41
Dances, 23, 51
Drums, 60

Education, 19, 23, 29-31, 38-39

Fiji
   animals, 16, 18, 43
   area, 14
   birds, 16, 18
   British colony, 12
   character of, 14-15
   Chinese in, 21
   climate, 14-15, 43-44
   crops, 37, 46, 47, 49
   education, 19, 29-31, 38-39
   government, 12-14

64

holidays, 51
Indians in, 19, 21
islands, 1-3, 15-16, 18
  formation of, 1, 3
languages in, 21, 29, 31, 38
legends, 56
location, 1
minerals, 47
money, 60
occupations in, 19, 21, 37, 38, 47
plants, 3, 16, 46, 47, 49
population, 16, 19
problems, social and economic,
  62-63
products, 46-47, 49
races in, 19, 21
Rotumans in, 21
schools, 19, 29-31, 38-39
villages, 14, 24, 25, 34, 35
Fijians
  characteristics of, 5, 15, 22-24
  chiefs, 10, 23, 24, 34, 42, 55
  clothing, 43-46
  crafts, 5
  food, 10-43
  languages, 29, 32
  recreation, 51-52
  sports, 49
  women, 44-45, 51, 52
Fire walking, 56-57
Fish drives, 50
Food
  Fijian, 40-43
  Indian, 43
Football, 49

Gasau, 25
Gold, 47
Government, Fiji, 12-14
Great Britain, 12

Hair styles, 22-23
Hindus, 19, 36, 43
Holidays, 51
Hurricanes, 15
Hymns, Methodist, 52

I Taukei, 19
Indians, 19, 20-21, 62-63
  characteristics of, 36, 37, 38
  clothing, 38
  education, 19, 38-39
  food, 43
  languages, 38
  settlements, 36-37
  sports, 49

Kerekere, 28
Korelevu, 62
Koro, 14

Lagoons, 1-2
Lali, 60
Land leasing, 19, 21, 47
Land rights, 19, 21
Languages, 21, 29, 31
  Fijian, 32
  Indian, 38
Lasakau, 34
Legends, Fijian, 56
"Long pig," 10

Macafu, 12, 34
Mandrai, 41
Manioc, 41
Market, open-air, 16
Medical School, Central, 31
Mekes, 51
Meke-wesi, 51
Melanesians, 3-5
Methodist church, 52

65

Minerals, 47
Missionaries
 Christian, 10, 45, 52
 Indian, 19
Money, Fijian, 60
"Mop tops," 23
Mount Victoria, 16
Muslims, 19, 36, 43

Nankeen cloth, 9
Newspapers, 21

Occupations, 19, 21, 29, 37, 38, 47

Plants, 3, 16, 46, 47, 49
Polynesians, 4-5
Population, 16, 19
Problems, social and economic,
 62-63
Products, export, 46-47, 49

Queen Victoria, 12, 51

Radio broadcasts, 21, 31
Railroad, narrow-gauge, 60
Rainfall, 15
Recreation, 49-52
Rivers, 16
Roko, 13
Rotumans, 21

Sandalwood, 6
Schools. *See* Education
Sea turtles, 16, 51, 56
Seashells, 62
Singing, group, 52

Soso, 34
Sports, 49
Sugar plantations, 19, 47
Sugarcane, 47, 60
Sulu, 43, 44
Suva, 16

Tabua, 9
Tapa cloth, 45-46
Taralala, 23
Tasman, Abel, 6
Taxes, 24, 36
Thatch, 25, 27
Tikinas, 13
Tourist business, 58, 60, 62
Traders, New England, 8-9

Vaka malolo, 51
Vanua Levu, 18
Villages, Fijian, 14, 24, 25, 34
 appearance, 25, 35
 council house, 25, 35
 location, 25
 work duties in, 24
Viti, 3
Viti Levu, 15-16, 58, 60
Volcanoes, 1, 14
Voting, 14, 21

Whale's teeth, 9
White-eyes, 18
Wilkes, Commander Charles, 6

Yaqona ceremony, 53-55
Yasanas, 13

Zebus, 43